GIGI

Gratitude Journal

30 DAYS TO A THANKFUL HEART

GIGI Gratitude Journal—30 days to a thankful heart

Published by 5 Sisters Ministry

P.O. BOX 6505, Upper Mt Gravatt, Australia 4122

Visit www.gigistorylibrary.com.au.

ISBN: 978-0-6454319-1-9

Copyright © 2022

Images used under licence from Depositphotos.com

Scripture taken from the Easy-to-Read Version® Copyright © 2006 by Bible League International. Used by permission. All rights reserved.

All rights reserved. No part of this publication may be reproduced, stored, or transmitted in any form without the written permission of the publisher-except for brief quotations in printed review.

GIGI
Gratitude
Journal

30 DAYS TO A THANKFUL HEART

5 Sisters Ministry
Brisbane, Australia

Hey GIGI girl,

God loves a thankful heart and there's nothing more beautiful than starting every day with gratitude. This journal is the perfect way for you to get into God's word while also thanking him for all He's done.

At the end of every 5 days, you can spend some time doing mindful colouring while playing your favourite worship songs in the background.

This daily gratitude journal will help you feel a lot happier, less anxious, and more at peace, because starting each day with God is everything.

Happy journaling!

Esther and Steph ♥

GIGI Co-founders

THIS JOURNAL BELONGS TO

_____

Date _____

VERSE OF THE DAY
1 Chronicles 16:34

_____

_____

_____

A person I am grateful for and why....

_____

_____

_____

_____

_____

_____

_____

_____

_____

_____

Write one highlight from yesterday....

_____

_____

_____

_____

_____

_____

_____

_____

Today I am grateful for....

I will turn off my phone for......
10 min   20 min   30 min   40min   _____

Something that makes me happy....

_____
_____
_____
_____
_____

One good deed I can do today....

_____
_____
_____
_____
_____

Dear Jesus, thank you for......

_____
_____
_____
_____
_____

Date _____

VERSE OF THE DAY
Psalm 105:1

_____

_____

_____

A person I am grateful for and why....   Write one highlight from yesterday....

Today I am grateful for....

I will turn off my phone for......
10 min   20 min   30 min   40min   _____

Something that makes me happy.... One good deed I can do today....

_____   _____
_____   _____
_____   _____
_____   _____
_____   _____

Dear Jesus, thank you for......

_____
_____
_____
_____
_____

Date _____

VERSE OF THE DAY
1 Thessalonians 5:18

_____

_____

_____

A person I am grateful for and why....   Write one highlight from yesterday....

Today I am grateful for....

I will turn off my phone for......
10 min   20 min   30 min   40min   _____

Something that makes me happy....

_____
_____
_____
_____
_____

One good deed I can do today....

_____
_____
_____
_____
_____

Dear Jesus, thank you for......

_____
_____
_____
_____
_____

Date _____

VERSE OF THE DAY
1 Chronicles 16:36

_____
_____
_____

A person I am grateful for and why....	Write one highlight from yesterday....

Today I am grateful for....

I will turn off my phone for......
10 min   20 min   30 min   40min   _____

Something that makes me happy....

_____

_____

_____

_____

One good deed I can do today....

_____

_____

_____

_____

Dear Jesus, thank you for......

_____

_____

_____

_____

_____

Date _____

VERSE OF THE DAY
Psalm 136:26

_____
_____
_____

A person I am grateful for and why....

_____
_____
_____
_____
_____
_____
_____
_____
_____
_____

Write one highlight from yesterday....

_____
_____
_____
_____
_____
_____
_____

Today I am grateful for....

I will turn off my phone for......
10 min   20 min   30 min   40min   _____

Something that makes me happy....
_____
_____
_____
_____
_____

One good deed I can do today....
_____
_____
_____
_____
_____

Dear Jesus, thank you for......
_____
_____
_____
_____
_____

Embellish your heart with the beauty of nature

Date _____

VERSE OF THE DAY
1 Chronicles 16:8

_____
_____
_____

A person I am grateful for and why....

Write one highlight from yesterday....

Today I am grateful for....

I will turn off my phone for......
10 min   20 min   30 min   40 min   _____

Something that makes me happy....
_____
_____
_____
_____
_____

One good deed I can do today....
_____
_____
_____
_____
_____

Dear Jesus, thank you for......
_____
_____
_____
_____
_____
_____

Date _____

VERSE OF THE DAY
Psalm 106:1

_____

_____

_____

A person I am grateful for and why....	Write one highlight from yesterday....
_____	_____
_____	_____
_____	_____
_____	_____
_____	_____
_____	_____
_____	_____
_____	_____
_____	
_____	

Today I am grateful for....

I will turn off my phone for......
10 min   20 min   30 min   40min   _____

Something that makes me happy....　　　　One good deed I can do today....

_____　　_____

_____　　_____

_____　　_____

_____　　_____

_____　　_____

Dear Jesus, thank you for......

_____

_____

_____

_____

_____

Date _____

VERSE OF THE DAY
Philippians 4:6

_____
_____
_____

A person I am grateful for and why....   Write one highlight from yesterday....

Today I am grateful for....

I will turn off my phone for......
10 min   20 min   30 min   40min   _____

Something that makes me happy....

_____
_____
_____
_____
_____

One good deed I can do today....

_____
_____
_____
_____
_____

Dear Jesus, thank you for......

_____
_____
_____
_____
_____

Date _____

VERSE OF THE DAY
1 Chronicles 16:28

_____

_____

_____

_____

A person I am grateful for and why....   Write one highlight from yesterday....

Today I am grateful for....

I will turn off my phone for......
10 min   20 min   30 min   40min   _____

Something that makes me happy....
_____
_____
_____
_____
_____

One good deed I can do today....
_____
_____
_____
_____
_____

Dear Jesus, thank you for......
_____
_____
_____
_____
_____

Date _____

VERSE OF THE DAY
Psalm 107:1

_____

_____

_____

A person I am grateful for and why....　　Write one highlight from yesterday....

Today I am grateful for....

I will turn off my phone for......
10 min   20 min   30 min   40min   _____

Something that makes me happy....
_____
_____
_____
_____
_____

One good deed I can do today....
_____
_____
_____
_____
_____

Dear Jesus, thank you for......
_____
_____
_____
_____
_____

Sparkle on the outside with how you take care of yourself through mind and body

Date _____

VERSE OF THE DAY
2 Corinthians 2:14

_____
_____
_____

A person I am grateful for and why....

_____
_____
_____
_____
_____
_____
_____
_____
_____

Write one highlight from yesterday....

_____
_____
_____
_____
_____
_____
_____

Today I am grateful for....

I will turn off my phone for......
10 min   20 min   30 min   40min   _____

Something that makes me happy....

_____
_____
_____
_____

One good deed I can do today....

_____
_____
_____
_____

Dear Jesus, thank you for......

_____
_____
_____
_____
_____

Date _____

VERSE OF THE DAY
Psalm 28:7

_____
_____
_____

A person I am grateful for and why....　　Write one highlight from yesterday....

Today I am grateful for....

I will turn off my phone for......
10 min   20 min   30 min   40min   _____

Something that makes me happy....

_____

_____

_____

_____

_____

One good deed I can do today....

_____

_____

_____

_____

_____

Dear Jesus, thank you for......

_____

_____

_____

_____

_____

Date _____

VERSE OF THE DAY
1 Chronicles 16:25

_____
_____
_____

A person I am grateful for and why.... | Write one highlight from yesterday....

Today I am grateful for....

I will turn off my phone for......
10 min   20 min   30 min   40min   _____

Something that makes me happy....

One good deed I can do today....

Dear Jesus, thank you for......

Date _____

VERSE OF THE DAY
Psalm 116:17

___

A person I am grateful for and why....

Write one highlight from yesterday....

Today I am grateful for....

I will turn off my phone for......
10 min   20 min   30 min   40min   _____

Something that makes me happy....

_____

_____

_____

_____

One good deed I can do today....

_____

_____

_____

_____

Dear Jesus, thank you for......

_____

_____

_____

_____

_____

Date _____

VERSE OF THE DAY
1 Corinthians 15:57

A person I am grateful for and why....

Write one highlight from yesterday....

Today I am grateful for....

I will turn off my phone for......
10 min   20 min   30 min   40min   _____

Something that makes me happy....

_____
_____
_____
_____
_____

One good deed I can do today....

_____
_____
_____
_____
_____

Dear Jesus, thank you for......

_____
_____
_____
_____
_____

Discover the true essence of your beauty

Date _____

VERSE OF THE DAY
1 Chronicles 16:9

_____
_____
_____

A person I am grateful for and why....   Write one highlight from yesterday....

Today I am grateful for....

I will turn off my phone for......
10 min   20 min   30 min   40min   _____

Something that makes me happy....

_____

_____

_____

_____

One good deed I can do today....

_____

_____

_____

_____

Dear Jesus, thank you for......

_____

_____

_____

_____

_____

Date _____

VERSE OF THE DAY
Psalm 95:2

_____
_____
_____

A person I am grateful for and why....   Write one highlight from yesterday....

Today I am grateful for....

I will turn off my phone for......
10 min   20 min   30 min   40min   _____

Something that makes me happy....
_____
_____
_____
_____
_____

One good deed I can do today....
_____
_____
_____
_____
_____

Dear Jesus, thank you for......
_____
_____
_____
_____
_____

Date _____

VERSE OF THE DAY
Colossians 3:15

___

A person I am grateful for and why....

Write one highlight from yesterday....

Today I am grateful for....

I will turn off my phone for......
10 min   20 min   30 min   40min   _____

Something that makes me happy....   One good deed I can do today....
_____   _____
_____   _____
_____   _____
_____   _____
_____   _____

Dear Jesus, thank you for......
_____
_____
_____
_____
_____

Date _____

VERSE OF THE DAY
Psalm 100:4

_____
_____
_____

A person I am grateful for and why....   Write one highlight from yesterday....

Today I am grateful for....

I will turn off my phone for......
10 min   20 min   30 min   40min   _____

Something that makes me happy....

_____

_____

_____

_____

One good deed I can do today....

_____

_____

_____

_____

Dear Jesus, thank you for......

_____

_____

_____

_____

_____

Date _____

VERSE OF THE DAY
1 Chronicles 23:30

_____

_____

_____

A person I am grateful for and why….　　　　Write one highlight from yesterday….

Today I am grateful for....

I will turn off my phone for......
10 min   20 min   30 min   40min   _____

Something that makes me happy....

_____

_____

_____

_____

_____

One good deed I can do today....

_____

_____

_____

_____

_____

Dear Jesus, thank you for......

_____

_____

_____

_____

_____

Allow God to direct your path and see your dreams soar

Date _____

VERSE OF THE DAY
Colossians 3:16

A person I am grateful for and why....

Write one highlight from yesterday....

Today I am grateful for....

I will turn off my phone for......
10 min   20 min   30 min   40min   _____

Something that makes me happy....
_____
_____
_____
_____
_____

One good deed I can do today....
_____
_____
_____
_____
_____

Dear Jesus, thank you for......
_____
_____
_____
_____
_____
_____

Date _____

VERSE OF THE DAY
Psalm 138:1

_____

_____

_____

A person I am grateful for and why....

Write one highlight from yesterday....

Today I am grateful for....

I will turn off my phone for......
10 min   20 min   30 min   40min   _____

Something that makes me happy....

_____

_____

_____

_____

One good deed I can do today....

_____

_____

_____

_____

Dear Jesus, thank you for......

_____

_____

_____

_____

_____

Date _____

VERSE OF THE DAY
1 Chronicles 16:23

_____
_____
_____

A person I am grateful for and why....

Write one highlight from yesterday....

Today I am grateful for....

I will turn off my phone for......
10 min   20 min   30 min   40min   _____

Something that makes me happy....

_____

_____

_____

_____

_____

One good deed I can do today....

_____

_____

_____

_____

_____

Dear Jesus, thank you for......

_____

_____

_____

_____

_____

Date _____

VERSE OF THE DAY
Colossians 3:17

_____
_____
_____

A person I am grateful for and why....   Write one highlight from yesterday....

Today I am grateful for....

I will turn off my phone for......
10 min   20 min   30 min   40min   _____

Something that makes me happy....

_____

_____

_____

_____

One good deed I can do today....

_____

_____

_____

_____

Dear Jesus, thank you for......

_____

_____

_____

_____

Date _____

VERSE OF THE DAY
Psalm 26:7

___

A person I am grateful for and why....

Write one highlight from yesterday....

Today I am grateful for....

I will turn off my phone for......
10 min   20 min   30 min   40min   _____

Something that makes me happy....
_____
_____
_____
_____
_____

One good deed I can do today....
_____
_____
_____
_____
_____

Dear Jesus, thank you for......
_____
_____
_____
_____
_____

Through your moments of pain and anxiety, find peace and healing with God

Date _____

VERSE OF THE DAY
1 Chronicles 29:13

A person I am grateful for and why....

Write one highlight from yesterday....

Today I am grateful for....

I will turn off my phone for......
10 min   20 min   30 min   40min   _____

Something that makes me happy....
_____
_____
_____
_____
_____

One good deed I can do today....
_____
_____
_____
_____
_____

Dear Jesus, thank you for......
_____
_____
_____
_____
_____

Date _____

VERSE OF THE DAY
Psalm 69:30

A person I am grateful for and why....

Write one highlight from yesterday....

Today I am grateful for....

I will turn off my phone for......
10 min   20 min   30 min   40min   _____

Something that makes me happy....

_____
_____
_____
_____
_____

One good deed I can do today....

_____
_____
_____
_____
_____

Dear Jesus, thank you for......

_____
_____
_____
_____
_____

Date _____

VERSE OF THE DAY
2 Corinthians 9:15

_____
_____
_____

A person I am grateful for and why....

Write one highlight from yesterday....

Today I am grateful for....

○
○
○

I will turn off my phone for......
10 min   20 min   30 min   40min   _____

Something that makes me happy....

_____
_____
_____
_____
_____

One good deed I can do today....

_____
_____
_____
_____
_____

Dear Jesus, thank you for......

_____
_____
_____
_____
_____

Date _____

VERSE OF THE DAY
Colossians 4:2

A person I am grateful for and why....   Write one highlight from yesterday....

Today I am grateful for....

I will turn off my phone for......
10 min   20 min   30 min   40 min   _____

Something that makes me happy....

_____
_____
_____
_____
_____

One good deed I can do today....

_____
_____
_____
_____
_____

Dear Jesus, thank you for......

_____
_____
_____
_____
_____

Date _____

VERSE OF THE DAY
1 Chronicles 16:31

___

A person I am grateful for and why....

Write one highlight from yesterday....

Today I am grateful for....

I will turn off my phone for......
10 min   20 min   30 min   40min   _____

Something that makes me happy....

_____
_____
_____
_____
_____

One good deed I can do today....

_____
_____
_____
_____
_____

Dear Jesus, thank you for......

_____
_____
_____
_____
_____
_____

Flourish knowing that you are God's beloved daughter

GIGI
Gorgeous in God's Image

www.ingramcontent.com/pod-product-compliance
Lightning Source LLC
Chambersburg PA
CBHW051158290426
44109CB00022B/2502